Caterpillar to Butterfly

Teaching Tips

Lilac Level 0

This book focuses on teaching the earliest readers how to read a book by following images and text from left to right.

Before Reading

- Discuss the title. Ask readers what they think the book will be about.

Read the Book

- Encourage readers to describe what they see on each page.
- Ask questions to help readers understand the story and its progression.
    - What happens at the beginning of the book?
    - What happens at the end of the book?
    - How do we know?

After Reading

- Ask readers what part of the book they liked best. Have them find the page or pages that showed this.
- Have readers imagine a different ending for the book. What else could have happened?

© 2024 Booklife Publishing
This edition is published by arrangement with Booklife Publishing.

North American adaptations © 2024 Jump!
5318 Penn Avenue South
Minneapolis, MN 55419
www.jumplibrary.com

Decodables by Jump! are published by Jump! Library.
All rights reserved. No part of this book may be reproduced in any form without written permission from the publisher.

Library of Congress Cataloging-in-Publication Data is available at www.loc.gov or upon request from the publisher.

ISBN: 979-8-88524-649-1 (hardcover)
ISBN: 979-8-88524-650-7 (paperback)
ISBN: 979-8-88524-651-4 (ebook)

Photo Credits

Images are courtesy of Shutterstock.com. With thanks to Getty Images, Thinkstock Photo and iStockphoto. Front Cover – Kim Pin, andregric. p4–5 – Sarah2, Kumbaya Photography. p6–7 – Marsha Mood, Liz Weber. p8–9 – Liz Weber, dossyl. p10–11 – ChameleonsEye, Visanuwit thongon.

About Reading

When we read a book, we go from left to right, like this:

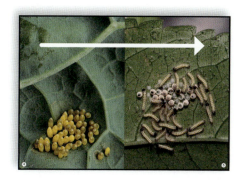

Some books just have pictures, like this:

Some books have words and pictures, like this:

Which of these steps comes first?

 Close the book and flip it over to read At the Dentist!

How do you brush your teeth?
Why do you brush your teeth?

 Close the book and flip it over to read Caterpillar to Butterfly!

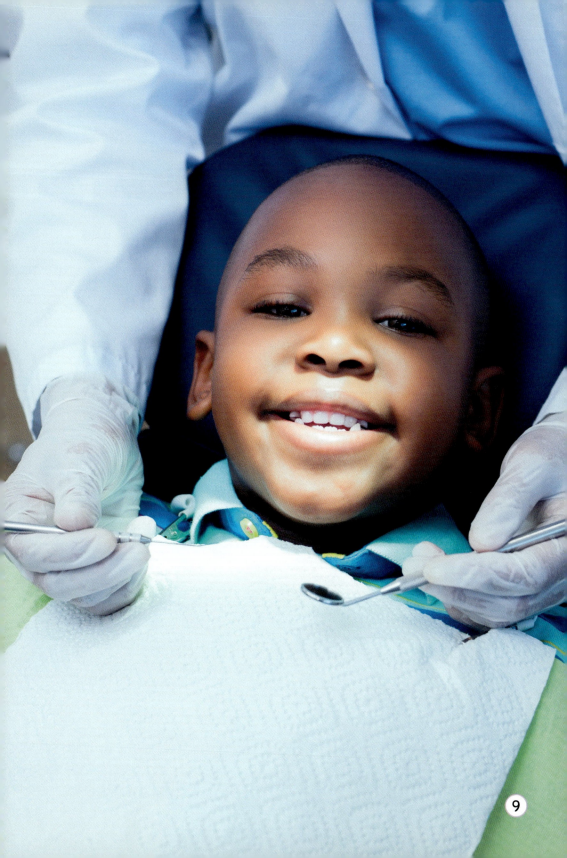

About Reading

When we read a book, we go from left to right, like this:

Some books just have pictures, like this:

Some books have words and pictures, like this:

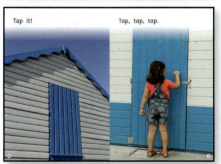

Teaching Tips

Lilac Level 0

This book focuses on teaching the earliest readers how to read a book by following images and text from left to right.

Before Reading

- Discuss the title. Ask readers what they think the book will be about.

Read the Book

- Encourage readers to describe what they see on each page.
- Ask questions to help readers understand the story and its progression.
    - What happens at the beginning of the book?
    - What happens at the end of the book?
    - How do we know?

After Reading

- Ask readers what part of the book they liked best. Have them find the page or pages that showed this.
- Have readers imagine a different ending for the book. What else could have happened?

© 2024 Booklife Publishing
This edition is published by arrangement with Booklife Publishing.

North American adaptations © 2024 Jump!
5318 Penn Avenue South
Minneapolis, MN 55419
www.jumplibrary.com

Decodables by Jump! are published by Jump! Library.
All rights reserved. No part of this book may be reproduced in any form without written permission from the publisher.

Library of Congress Cataloging-in-Publication Data is available at www.loc.gov or upon request from the publisher.

ISBN: 979-8-88524-649-1 (hardcover)
ISBN: 979-8-88524-650-7 (paperback)
ISBN: 979-8-88524-651-4 (ebook)

Photo Credits
Images are courtesy of Shutterstock.com. With thanks to SuperStock, Getty Images, Thinkstock Photo and iStockphoto. Cover– wavebreakmedia, BrunoWeltmann, Africa Studio, Bozena Fulawka. p4–5– TY Lim, Peathegee Inc/Blend Images. p6–7– wavebreakmedia, XiXinXing. p8–9– wavebreakmedia. p10–11– AboutLife, gorillaimages.

At the Dentist